W9-AQT-533

by Marion Downer

LONG AGO IN FLORENCE

The Story of the della Robbia Sculpture

Illustrated with museum photographs

DRAWINGS BY MAMORU FUNAI

Lothrop, Lee & Shepard Co., Inc.
NEW YORK

Also by Marion Downer

ROOFS OVER AMERICA
THE STORY OF DESIGN
DISCOVERING DESIGN
KITES—How to Make and Fly Them

Library of Congress Catalog Card Number: 68-27707 *Printed in the United States of America*

1 2 3 4 5 72 71 70 69 68

For the children

The city of Florence, in Italy, was known for its natural beauty. In the fifteenth century many artists worked there and added their art to its fame. One of them was the sculptor Luca della Robbia. Luca had a ground-floor studio that opened onto a wide courtyard surrounded by a brick wall with trees growing close to it and vines climbing over it. On the studio floor large blocks of marble–some as tall as Luca himself–always stood ready for use.

Luca worked with a chisel in one hand and a mallet in the other, and as he shaved off the pieces of marble and carved the shape he wanted to make, he scattered chips from one end of the studio to the other.

Neighbor children often came to visit Luca. They liked to sing and play games, scuffing around in the marble dust that covered the floor of the big studio. And Luca liked to have them there. He was fond of children and took inspiration from them. He worked with special care on the head of a child and polished it lovingly. Sometimes he stopped work entirely, sat on a chunk of marble, and encouraged the boys and girls to sing for him and talk about the things that interested them.

A panel of the *Cantoria*, or Singing Gallery, by Luca della Robbia. Marble, 15th century Florentine Italian. Museum of S. Maria del Fiore, Florence. *Alinari-Art Reference Bureau.*

When a great Italian cathedral needed marble sculpture to ornament its choir loft, Luca was one of the sculptors invited to do the work. Naturally, Luca's idea for his part included children. He carved large rectangular pieces of marble with figures in high relief. Most of the figures were of boys and girls playing musical instruments, dancing and singing hymns. They looked a great deal like the children who so often visited Luca.

Luca often worked late into the night in his big studio. During the winter it was so cold there that he sat with his feet in a basket of wood shavings to keep them warm while he made drawings of the things he wanted to sculpture. He also modeled little figures in wax for practice. He wanted to be sure that his statues always had perfectly natural proportions and were made in lifelike positions.

Luca had no wife or children of his own, but he was especially fond of his brother's two small sons, Andrea and Simone. Sometimes they came to visit him in his studio. Ever since Andrea was about eleven years old, they had all lived together in a large stone house Luca had bought and where he had his studio.

During the fifteenth century nearly all art was commissioned by rich men for homes or churches. Luca was asked to make sculptured altar pieces and figures for framed niches. The Italian people, who loved art, greatly admired his work.

However, Luca was not a rich man. He could not give away work made of costly marble that took a great deal of time to carve. And only the handsome city cathedrals could afford to buy heavy marble or bronze sculpture.

But Luca had found a way to make something beautiful that even simple little country churches could afford to buy. For some time he had been working on a method for making sculpture that was both easy and inexpensive. He planned to make it, not of marble, but of terra-cotta.

In Italian, the word terra-cotta means cooked clay. Clay saved Luca a great deal of time because it was so easy to model. He had a special furnace with a brick oven built in his yard, and there he fired the large pieces of clay sculpture for days at a time.

Madonna and Child with Six Angels by Luca della Robbia. Terra-cotta, 15th century Florentine Italian. *The Detroit Institute of Art.*

The first clay sculpture Luca made in his furnace was dull in color and did not quite please him. The clay needed a hard, glossy covering to give it a pleasing and lasting finish.

Luca had to find a way to give color to the surface. Enamel glaze was what he wanted. But in the fifteenth century enamel was confined to clay pottery. The ancient Chinese, the Persians, and the Babylonians had all made colored enamel, and the Arabs had brought the secret to Europe, but no one knew how to use it on large clay figures.

Madonna and Child by Luca della Robbia. Glazed terra-cotta, 15th century Florentine Italian. *Albright-Knox Art Gallery, Buffalo, N.Y. Seymour H. Knox Fund.*

Luca found old books in libraries that told how enamel glaze was once made. Finally, by 1441, he had developed a mixture that would adhere to clay and, when baked, take on a bright lustre.

Luca often used several colors of this enamel on his terra-cotta sculptures, but he preferred to use just blue and white when he made a Madonna and Child.

By this time Luca needed an artist to help him in his studio, and his nephew Andrea was old enough to be trained in the work. Andrea learned quickly. He was clever with his hands and could follow directions. Luca continued to design the enameled terra-cotta pieces, but he gave Andrea a chance to model and fire terra-cotta sculpture himself. Soon Andrea's skill was almost equal to his uncle's.

Luca hired workmen to assist him in baking his terra-cotta figures, and the della Robbia studio began to be a very busy place. A number of small churches were able to pay the low price he charged for enameled terra-cotta sculpture. They bought plaques for their bare walls, and they placed lunettes over their doorways. They put up statues in their gardens and sometimes in wayside shrines among cypress trees and vines.

Neither rain, nor sun, nor freezing cold could injure Luca's beautiful enamel.

Madonna of the Dicite by Luca della Robbia. Enameled terra-cotta, 15th century Florentine Italian. *The Museum of Fine Arts, Boston.*

The della Robbia workshop must have been a happy place. Everyone could sing at his work if he felt like it, and at noon an aroma of good Italian cooking floated in from Luca's kitchen. Then all the workers sat down to eat and, after a short rest, went back to work again.

The pieces of terra-cotta sculpture they made were often marked "From the della Robbia workshop," but no matter who had done the work on them, Luca was the genius behind everything the studio produced.

Head of a Youth by Andrea della Robbia. Glazed terra-cotta, 15th century Florentine Italian. *The Detroit Institute of Art.*

Distinguished noblemen sometimes gave Luca orders for terra-cotta plaques to ornament their castles. Some of the men liked wreaths with colored leaves and fruit. Some of them liked to have their coat of arms copied into the middle of the wreaths. Others admired portrait heads of themselves set within decorative borders.

As Luca grew older Andrea had more and more to do with the art works that came out of the studio. But Luca's influence remained.

Luca della Robbia never lost his love of children or his desire to use them as models, and he invited them into his studio when there was a lull in the work.

One day, when it had grown late, a mother, carrying an infant in her arms, came to call her children home, and Luca asked her to sit down and rest. He had some grapes and cakes brought to his guest and then picked up his drawing pad. As was the custom then, the baby was wrapped in swaddling clothes with only its arms free to move. As the mother held the child up, Luca made sketches.

First *Bambino* by Andrea della Robbia. Glazed terra-cotta, 15th century Florentine Italian. *Alinari-Art Reference Bureau.*

Not long afterward a request came to the workshop from the Hospital of the Innocents in Florence. The hospital, which was a home for little children who had no mothers or fathers, was being enlarged, and Luca was commissioned to do ten terra-cotta plaques, to be set in a row across the portico of the building.

Luca planned for each plaque to be a circle with the figure of an infant, or bambino as the Italians say, in its center. Each bambino was to be in swaddling clothes like the one Luca had drawn in his studio.

The ten plaques were made, but not by Luca. He was now a very old man and did not have the strength to undertake such a big job. So Andrea made them all.

Andrea's circular plaques have been admired and loved for centuries. Many copies of them have been made and they hang on walls all over the world. In Florence people often go to see the row of plaques. The sculptured bambinos seem to hold out their arms, each one asking to be cared for and loved.

Second *Bambino* by Andrea della Robbia. Glazed terra-cotta, 15th century Florentine Italian. *Alinari-Art Reference Bureau.*

A group of boys and girls who had played in Luca's workshop when they were small children came to his gates one day and stood there reverently. Luca had died and the gates were closed out of respect for him.

As time passed Andrea carried on with the work of the studio.

After Luca's death works of art continued to come from the della Robbia workshop. Andrea had four sons who also took part in making enameled terra-cotta. The most talented of them was Giovanni, who is said to have made the sculptured bust of a child, sometimes called The Boy St. John.

Head of a Youth in a medalion by Andrea della Robbia. Glazed terra-cotta, 15th century Italian.

The Metropolitan Museum of Art, Rogers Fund, 1903.

The Archangel Michael, lunette from San Michele Archangelo, Faenza, by Andrea della Robbia. Enameled terra-cotta, c. 1475, Italian.
The Metropolitan Museum of Art, Harris Brisbane Dick Fund, 1960.

The younger della Robbias kept the workshop open for many years. But no one in the family ever inherited the genius of Luca. No one ever sculptured children with quite as much accuracy and feeling as he did–as if each child was his own beloved friend.

The serene figure of the Madonna and Child is typical of Luca's finest terra-cotta sculpture. Now several centuries old, it stands in a gallery of the Metropolitan Museum in New York City.

Placed high against a wall of the gallery and decorated in gleaming white and blue, its graceful shape

Madonna and Child with Scroll by Luca della Robbia. Enameled terra-cotta, 15th century Florentine Italian. *The Metropolitan Museum of Art, Bequest of Benjamin Altman, 1913.*

accents the room. Silently it tells of Luca della Robbia's lasting greatness.

He was a true originator. All that he did was new in his time–long, long ago in Florence.